NATIONAL GEOGRAPHIC KiDS

PUZZLE BOOK

HOLIDAY

FACT-PACKED FUN

CONTENTS

Getting there

Get prepared for fun facts and puzzles about holidays. Read on to find out more.

HEATHROW AIRPORT in **LONDON** is used by over **75 MILLION PASSENGERS** every year.

CROSSWORDS

Crack the crosswords to start the fuel pump by solving the cryptic clues below.
Answers have the same amount of letters as the number in brackets.
Can you work out the travel keyword using the letters in the shaded squares?
See if you are right by flicking to page 90.

Across

1   Put back in position (7)
6   The number after six (5)
7   Premiership football team that plays at Anfield (9)
8   Last match in a tournament (5)
9   Where you catch a train from (7)

Down

1   Daniel ___ : actor who played Harry Potter (9)
2   Country where one finds Sydney (9)
3   Jealous (7)
4   Polite name for a male (9)
5   Money set aside for later use (7)

The **PETROL** that we use to **FUEL** cars comes from oil that's found **DEEP DOWN UNDER THE EARTH.**

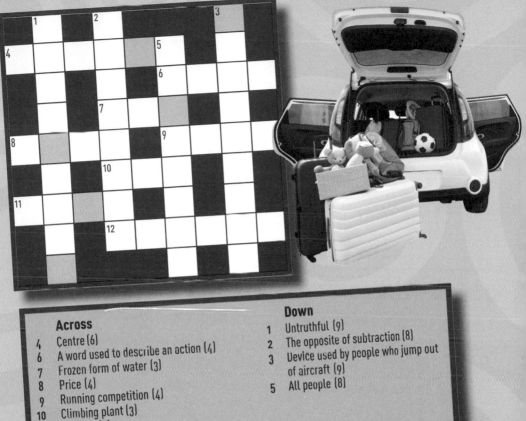

Across

4. Centre (6)
6. A word used to describe an action (4)
7. Frozen form of water (3)
8. Price (4)
9. Running competition (4)
10. Climbing plant (3)
11. Nothing (4)
12. The number 90 (6)

Down

1. Untruthful (9)
2. The opposite of subtraction (8)
3. Device used by people who jump out of aircraft (9)
5. All people (8)

A car's **SAT NAV SYSTEM** gets directions by exchanging messages with a **SATELLITE IN SPACE.**

SUDOKUS

Solve the sudokus to get your train ticket.
Fill in the blank squares so that numbers 1 to 6 appear once in each row,
column and 3x2 box. See if you are right by flicking to page 90.

1	6				
	2	4		3	
			2	4	5
4		2			
	4				
2				1	4

← 16 発車ご案内
Train Departures

列車名 Train	列車番号 Train No.	時刻 Time	行先 Destination
		9:33 Shin-Ōsaka	Non-Reserved Car No.1–5
This train stops at:	Shinagawa, Shin-Yokohama, Odawara, Nagoya, Gifu-Hashima, Maibara, Kyōto		
KODAMA 645		9:56 Shin-Ōsaka	Non-Reserved Car No.1–7,14,15
This train stops at:	All stations		
NOZOMI 165		10:40 Hakata	Non-Reserved Car No.1–3

Puzzle 1

3			1	6	5	2
				3		
5						3
	3					6
1			3			
2				1		5

Puzzle 2

			1		4
4			2	5	
	1		4		
				2	1
1	3			4	2
6		4		1	

Wordsearches

Scour the airport to find the airport terms. Search left to right, up and down to find the words listed in the boxes below. See if you are right by flicking to page 90.

cabin crew	pilot
check-in	runway
duty free	take off
luggage	transfer
passport	travel

THE QUEEN doesn't own **A PASSPORT** and doesn't need one to travel, but the rest of the **ROYAL FAMILY** do.

EUROPEAN UNION

UNITED KINGDOM OF GREAT BRITAIN AND NORTHERN IRELAND

DIEU ET MON DROIT

PASSPORT

t	i	q	y	k	i	w	t	m	c
r	c	e	i	r	s	e	p	t	a
a	c	a	a	u	a	t	a	r	b
v	s	t	u	n	t	a	s	a	i
e	a	s	u	w	t	k	s	n	n
l	u	g	g	a	g	e	p	s	c
t	r	o	e	y	j	o	o	f	r
e	y	d	u	t	y	f	r	e	e
t	p	i	l	o	t	f	t	r	w
c	h	e	c	k	i	n	t	f	p

DUTY FREE 🎁 →

airline
games
gate
help desk
journey

security
shuttle bus
snacks
suitcase
tickets

s	h	h	t	i	c	k	e	t	s
n	e	j	o	u	r	n	e	y	h
a	l	a	e	v	z	l	p	g	u
c	p	c	r	s	r	m	s	a	t
k	d	r	e	i	r	j	b	m	t
s	e	c	u	r	i	t	y	e	l
r	s	s	u	i	t	c	a	s	e
i	k	l	g	a	t	e	o	i	b
f	i	s	e	a	m	r	x	r	u
a	a	i	r	l	i	n	e	a	s

BOARDING PASS
PASSENGER TICKET AND BAGGAGE CHECK

GATE	GATE CLOSES	SEAT
7	19:30	25 b

Class
First Class

Departure
New York

Arrival
Paris

R No
023 07654 00984

BOARDING PASS
FIRST CLASS

GATE: 7

GATE CLOSES: 19:30

SEAT 25 b

13

SPOT THE DIFFERENCE

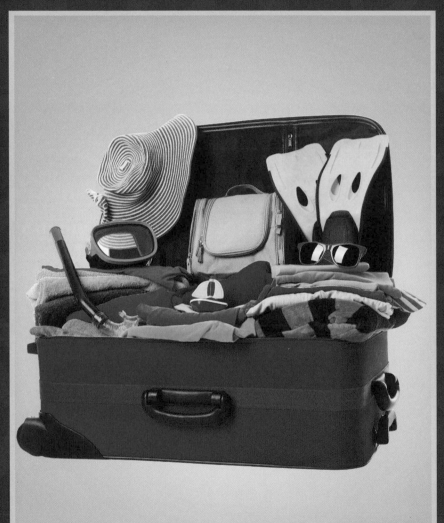

Compare the two images of the suitcase.
Can you spot the five differences between the images?
See if you are right by flicking to page 91.

'SMARTCASES'
are **SUITCASES** that
use **TECHNOLOGY** like
built-in scales, usb ports for
charging, and solar power
batteries.

15

GUESS WHAT?

Can you guess the answers to the travel questions below?
Check your guesses by flicking to page 91.

1. What document should be presented at passport control?
   a) Birth certificate
   b) Passport
   c) Boarding pass

2. What part of a plane do animals travel in?
   a) In the hold
   b) On your lap
   c) In the wings

3. How many terminals are there at Heathrow airport?
   a) 1
   b) 5
   c) 7

4. In 2016, which was the busiest airport?
   a) Dubai International
   b) London Heathrow
   c) Hartsfield–Jackson Atlanta International

5. How many passengers used London Heathrow in 2016?
   a) 75.7 million
   b) 94.2 million
   c) 34.8 million

6. Where is the smallest airport in the world?
   a) Saba Airport, Caribbean
   b) Luang Prabang, Laos
   c) Barra Airport, Scotland

7. What would allow you to carry more luggage on your car?
   a) Door rack
   b) Bonnet rack
   c) Roof rack

8. Modern cars have a navigation system controlled by:
   a) Satellites
   b) Stars
   c) Magnets

9. Train times are usually displayed on:
   a) Newspapers
   b) Billboards
   c) Departure boards

10) Train tickets are usually checked by the:
   a) Inspector
   b) Conductor
   c) Invigilator

Work your way around the maze until you reach the exit.
See if you are right by flicking to page 91.

MAZE

Word wheels

Can you work out the travel items
in the two word wheels?
See if you are right by flicking to page 91.

At the beach

Dive into this chapter for sun, sea and seriously fun facts and puzzles from the seaside.

THE TALLEST SANDCASTLE ever built was over **16 METRES HIGH** and took nearly **A MONTH TO BUILD!**

CROSSWORDS

Crack the crosswords before hitting the beach by solving the cryptic clues below.
Answers have the same amount of letters as the number in brackets.
Can you work out the beach keyword using the letters in the shaded squares?
See if you are right by flicking to page 92.

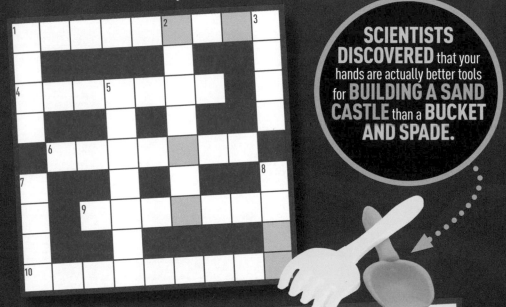

SCIENTISTS **DISCOVERED** that your hands are actually better tools for **BUILDING A SAND CASTLE** than a **BUCKET AND SPADE.**

Across

1 A two-wheeled vehicle with an engine (9)
4 Details of where you live (7)
6 Image (7)
9 The number 16 (7)
10 Exciting trip (9)

Down

1 Unkind (4)
2 Cookie (7)
3 Jealousy (4)
5 Be presented with (7)
7 Tiny insect; leaf (anag) (4)
8 A single time (4)

The most expensive **SUNGLASSES** sold on **EBAY** once belonged to **ELVIS PRESLEY** and were sold for over **£180,000.**

Across

1 Popular school sport (7)
6 Not clear; indistinct (5)
7 Letters that are not capital letters (5,4)
8 The Queen's favourite type of dog (5)
9 A particular kind of organism (7)

Down

1 Piece of jewellery (9)
2 Market a product (9)
3 Baggage (7)
4 These are made from beaten eggs cooked in frying pans (9)
5 Opposite of downwards (7)

SUDOKUS

Solve the sudokus before tucking into your fish and chips.
Fill in the blank squares so that numbers 1 to 6 appear once in each row,
column and 3x2 box. See if you are right by flicking to page 92.

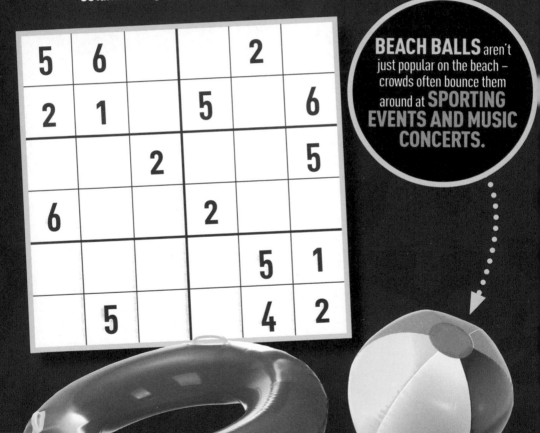

5	6			2	
2	1		5		6
		2			5
6			2		
				5	1
	5			4	2

BEACH BALLS aren't
just popular on the beach –
crowds often bounce them
around at **SPORTING
EVENTS AND MUSIC
CONCERTS.**

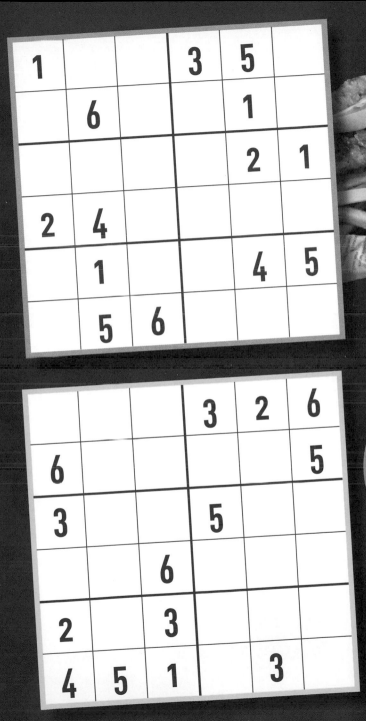

Until the **1980s,** it was traditional for **FISH AND CHIPS** to always be served **WRAPPED IN NEWSPAPER.**

Wordsearches

Explore the beach and uncover the beach terms.
Search left to right, up and down to find the words listed in the boxes below.
See if you are right by flicking to page 92.

s	g	d	h	b	r	a	x	s	j
u	t	e	r	e	u	v	b	a	q
n	q	c	t	a	b	i	g	n	o
b	b	k	x	c	b	c	l	d	h
l	u	c	s	h	e	e	a	a	e
o	c	h	t	t	r	c	s	l	s
c	k	a	u	o	r	r	s	s	p
k	e	i	o	w	i	e	e	n	a
x	t	r	c	e	n	a	s	q	d
l	i	l	o	l	g	m	a	l	e

VANILLA is considered the most popular **ICE CREAM FLAVOUR IN THE WORLD,** closely **FOLLOWED BY CHOCOLATE.**

beach towel
bucket
deckchair
glasses
ice cream

lilo
rubber ring
sandals
spade
sunblock

s	s	y	e	s	h	e	l	l	s	s
u	j	n	a	s	h	i	d	f	a
r	e	h	y	c	p	t	e	c	n
f	l	i	f	e	g	u	a	r	d
b	l	r	b	t	m	h	p	t	c
o	y	p	e	b	b	l	e	l	a
a	f	l	i	p	f	l	o	p	s
r	i	s	w	i	m	s	u	i	t
d	s	y	p	a	r	a	s	o	l
a	h	p	a	l	m	t	r	e	e

flip-flops

jellyfish

lifeguard

palm tree

parasol

pebble

sandcastle

shells

surfboard

swimsuit

IN CROYDE, ENGLAND, there is a CINEMA where all of the SEATS have been replaced with DECKCHAIRS.

SPOT THE DIFFERENCE

Compare the two images of the beach scene.
Can you spot the five differences between the images?
See if you are right by flicking to page 93.

FLIP-FLOPS are called 'JAPONKI' IN POLAND, 'SLOPS' IN SOUTH AFRICA, and 'THONGS' IN AUSTRALIA!

GUESS WHAT?

Can you guess the answers to the beach questions below?
Check your guesses by flicking to page 93.

1. **What does a blue flag at a beach usually represent?**
   a) A dangerous beach with lots of hazards
   b) A beach for adults only
   c) A safe and clean beach

2. **What is a group of whales called?**
   a) A pod
   b) A plod
   c) A prod

3. **What do you traditionally eat ice cream from?**
   a) A mug
   b) A cone
   c) A tray

4. **What is the main purpose of a parasol at a sunny beach?**
   a) To shield you from the sun
   b) To deter seagulls
   c) To attract the sun

5) **What does sunblock protect your skin from?**
   a) UV rays from the sun
   b) Water exposure
   c) Wind chills

6. **Which of these towns in Cornwall is famous for its beaches?**
   a) Oldquay
   b) Modernquay
   c) Newquay

7. **What do you traditionally make out of sand when at the beach?**
   a) Sand balls
   b) Sand dunes
   c) Sandcastles

8. **How many arms do starfish usually have?**
   a) 3
   b) 4
   c) 5

9. **Which of these might you encounter walking along the beach?**
   a) Rock pool
   b) Stone pool
   c) Pebble pool

10. **What name is given to the sport of riding waves whilst on a board?**
    a) Parkour
    b) Surfing
    c) Zorbing

MAZE

Work your way around the
maze until you reach the exit.
See if you are right by flicking to page 93.

Word wheels

Can you work out the beach words
in the two word wheels?
See if you are right by flicking to page 93.

City break

Are you ready for the hustle and bustle of a city break? Start your adventure here, for fun facts and puzzles.

A LONDON CAB traditionally has to be tall enough to be a **COMFORTABLE RIDE** for somebody wearing a **BOWLER HAT.**

CROSSWORDS

Crack the crosswords to board the double decker by solving the cryptic clues below.
Answers have the same amount of letters as the number in brackets.
Can you work out the city break keyword using the letters in the shaded squares?
See if you are right by flicking to page 94.

Across

1 ___ Day: 25th December (9)
4 Dessert (7)
6 Sour liquid put on chips (7)
9 Far away (7)
10 Attractive insect with colourful wings (9)

Down

1 Mimic; imitate (4)
2 This evening (7)
3 Move through water (4)
5 Person who looks after teeth (7)
7 Toothed object used for styling hair (4)
8 Remain in place (4)

The first ever
LONDON BUS
service was a carriage that
was pulled by **THREE HORSES.**

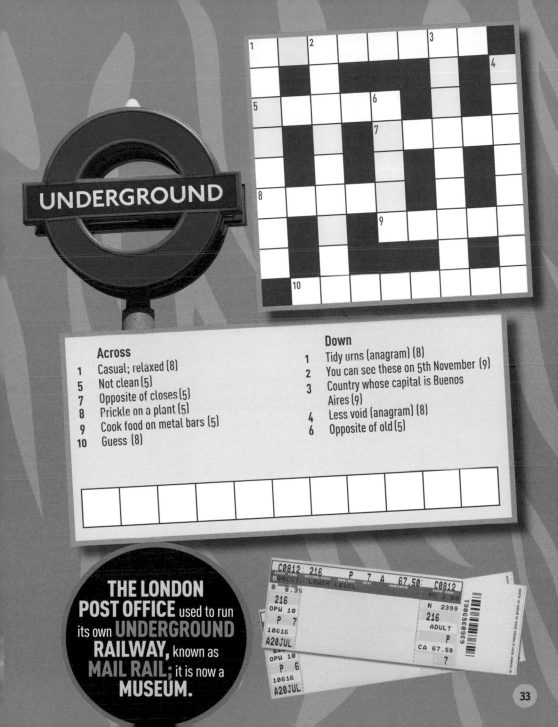

Across
1 Casual; relaxed (8)
5 Not clean (5)
7 Opposite of closes (5)
8 Prickle on a plant (5)
9 Cook food on metal bars (5)
10 Guess (8)

Down
1 Tidy urns (anagram) (8)
2 You can see these on 5th November (9)
3 Country whose capital is Buenos Aires (9)
4 Less void (anagram) (8)
6 Opposite of old (5)

THE LONDON POST OFFICE used to run its own **UNDERGROUND RAILWAY,** known as **MAIL RAIL;** it is now a **MUSEUM.**

SUDOKUS

Solve the sudokus to pay your taxi fare.
Fill in the blank squares so that numbers 1 to 6 appear once in each row,
column and 3x2 box. See if you are right by flicking to page 94.

		1		2	6
	5	4			
		3	5	6	4
2	3		4	5	1

There are currently over **13,000 YELLOW TAXICABS** in the **CITY OF NEW YORK.**

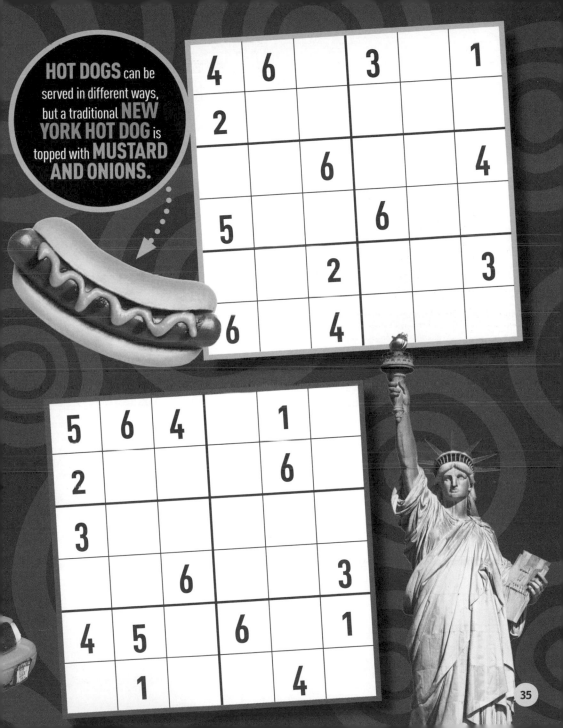

HOT DOGS can be served in different ways, but a traditional NEW YORK HOT DOG is topped with MUSTARD AND ONIONS.

Puzzle 1 (top grid):

4	6		3		1
2					
		6			4
5			6		
		2			3
6		4			

Puzzle 2 (bottom grid):

5	6	4		1	
2				6	
3					
		6			3
4	5		6		1
	1			4	

Wordsearches

Look out for the city break terms as you explore Paris.
Search left to right, up and down to find the words listed in the boxes below.
See if you are right by flicking to page 94.

People from **NEW YORK CITY** drink nearly **SEVEN TIMES MORE COFFEE** than people from anywhere else in the **USA**.

a	g	v	t	c	s	f	s	a	c
c	n	i	o	u	m	e	t	r	o
a	a	e	u	l	e	m	m	l	f
m	r	w	r	t	d	o	u	u	f
e	j	p	b	u	a	n	s	l	e
r	t	o	u	r	g	u	i	d	e
a	v	i	s	e	m	m	g	s	s
p	u	n	o	k	q	e	h	t	g
i	r	t	d	g	d	n	t	u	y
t	o	u	r	i	s	t	s	m	k

camera

coffee

culture

metro

monument

sights

tour bus

tour guide

tourists

viewpoint

u	w	a	l	k	i	n	g	z	q
a	c	r	o	w	d	s	m	o	p
r	s	o	u	v	e	n	i	r	s
e	x	p	e	r	i	e	n	c	e
s	d	s	h	o	p	p	i	n	g
e	s	s	b	t	h	e	b	i	s
a	a	t	h	i	p	e	r	m	c
r	c	a	f	e	u	r	e	c	r
c	t	l	a	n	d	m	a	r	k
h	p	i	c	n	i	c	k	o	u

METRO

cafe
crowds
experience
landmark
mini-break

picnic
research
shopping
souvenirs
walking

Compare the two images of Central Park.
Can you spot the five differences between the images?
See if you are right by flicking to page 95.

NEW YORK'S CENTRAL PARK, the most visited **URBAN PARK IN THE USA,** has over 9,000 benches!

GUESS WHAT?

Can you guess the answers to the city break questions below?
Check your guesses by flicking to page 95.

1. Which of these is a famous transport system in Paris?
   a) Motto
   b) Metro
   c) Pogo

2) What is the name of someone who shows people around a city?
   a) Tourist
   b) Tour point
   c) Tour guide

3. Which of these is a famous park in New York?
   a) Middle Park
   b) Left Park
   c) Central Park

4. If you went on a city break to the German capital, which city would you visit?
   a) Frankfurt
   b) Munich
   c) Berlin

5) Where in Italy would you find lots of gondolas?
   a) Florence
   b) Pisa
   c) Venice

6. What colour are London's famous taxis?
   a) Yellow
   b) Red
   c) Black

7. How much money on average is thrown in to the Trevi Fountain in Rome every day?
   a) £26
   b) £260
   c) £2,600

8. Which of these is a famous department store in New York?
   a) Karen's
   b) Sharon's
   c) Macy's

9. What is New York also known as?
   a) The curvy pear
   b) The juicy orange
   c) The big apple

10. Where would you find the Eiffel Tower?
    a) Paris
    b) London
    c) Barcelona

Work your way around the maze
until you reach the exit.
See if you are right by flicking to page 95.

MAZE

Word wheels

Can you work out the city break words
in the two word wheels?
See if you are right by flicking to page 95.

OneStep
closeup

Word wheel 1: N P H S I O G P

Word wheel 2: T E H A R T E

On safari

Hold on tight! Beware of fun facts and puzzles on all things safari in this chapter.

LIONS are the **SECOND FASTEST WILD CATS,** they can run at speeds of up to **50 MILES PER HOUR!**

CROSSWORDS

Help the safari animals crack the crosswords by solving the cryptic clues below.
Answers have the same amount of letters as the number in brackets.
Can you work out the safari keyword using the letters in the shaded squares?
See if you are right by flicking to page 96.

Across

4　Turn into (6)
6　Use your eyes (4)
7　Sharp nail of an animal (4)
8　Make better (4)
9　A sweet fruit with a distinctive shape (4)
10　Chess piece that can jump over other pieces (6)

Down

1　Necklaces and rings, for instance (9)
2　Task a teacher asks you to do away from school (8)
3　School subject (9)
5　____ eel: type of fish (8)

There are three species of **ZEBRAS** in the world: plains, mountain, and Grévy's zebras. **ALL OF THEM LIVE IN AFRICA.**

Across

4. Direction of this crossword clue (6)
6. Way out (4)
7. Where you are right now (4)
8. Very small (4)
9. Mars (anagram) (4)
10. Reason given to justify a fault (6)

Down

1. Object in a field that frightens birds (9)
2. Rubbish (8)
3. E.g. Einstein or Newton (9)
5. String of words that mean something (8)

RHINOS are known for their **GIANT, MAGNIFICENT HORNS.** The name **'RHINOCEROS'** literally means **'NOSE HORN.'**

SUDOKUS

Solve the sudokus before setting off on safari.
Fill in the blank squares so that numbers 1 to 6 appear once in each row,
column and 3x2 box. See if you are right by flicking to page 96.

A **HIPPO'S EYES AND NOSE** are on top of its head so it can **SEE AND BREATHE** while keeping cool submerged in water.

4	2	6			
			2		
6	5	2			4
3				6	
5		3		2	
			4		5

46

Puzzle 1

3	1	6			
	5		6		
			2	1	
	6	2			
		1		5	2
		3			4

Because vultures have a **GREAT SENSE OF SMELL**, some can **DETECT METHANE** leaks in gas lines.

Puzzle 2

6	2	1		5	
	3		6	1	2
					1
5					
		4		6	
			2	4	

Wordsearches

Grab your binoculars and spot the safari terms. Search left to right, up and down to find the words listed in the boxes below. See if you are right by flicking to page 96.

antelope
cheetah
elephant
giraffe
gorilla

hyena
meerkat
parrot
rhino
sloth

GIRAFFES have very **LONG TONGUES** which can grow to over **50 CM,** and help them to eat leaves from **HIGH BRANCHES.**

q	e	k	n	z	k	r	r	u	a
o	s	l	o	s	t	x	e	a	b
s	l	m	e	e	r	k	a	t	a
g	o	r	i	l	l	a	d	p	l
j	t	c	h	e	e	t	a	h	w
c	h	t	j	p	a	r	r	o	t
t	t	d	r	h	i	n	o	r	v
s	g	i	r	a	f	f	e	s	s
g	h	y	e	n	a	r	r	e	t
u	e	a	n	t	e	l	o	p	e

ELEPHANTS have very **SENSITIVE FEET,** which they can use to **'HEAR' VIBRATIONS** through the ground.

r	w	e	v	r	s	z	q	c	s
g	a	z	e	l	l	e	d	i	f
c	r	o	c	o	d	i	l	e	a
t	t	s	m	o	n	k	e	y	f
s	h	t	b	a	b	o	o	n	x
i	o	r	v	i	e	h	p	x	z
a	g	i	d	o	s	n	a	k	e
s	o	c	a	z	b	f	r	u	b
q	o	h	l	i	o	n	d	n	r
p	x	s	s	u	l	k	t	s	a

baboon
crocodile
gazelle
leopard
lion

monkey
ostrich
snake
warthog
zebra

49

CLOSE UP

Match the mind-boggling magnifications to the named pictures opposite. See if you are right by flicking to page 97.

1

2

3

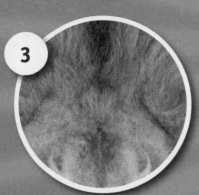

4

5

6

Lion

1

Zebra

2

Giraffe

3

Elephant

4

Flamingo

5

6 Crocodile

51

GUESS WHAT?

Can you guess the answers to the safari questions below?
Check your guesses by flicking to page 97.

1. Safaris show animals in:
   a) Captivity
   b) Rehabilitation
   c) Their natural environment

2. What colour are a zebra's stripes?
   a) Black and white
   b) Green and gold
   c) Blue and white

3. Which animal is the fastest?
   a) Cheetah
   b) Gazelle
   c) Hyena

4. Which animal is the tallest?
   a) Elephant
   b) Giraffe
   c) Buffalo

5. What are female buffalos called?
   a) Does
   b) Calfs
   c) Cows

6. A popular destination for safaris is:
   a) Kosovo
   b) Kuwait
   c) Kenya

7. What are a group of lions called?
   a) A pack
   b) A herd
   c) A pride

8. Where is Kruger National Park?
   a) Botswana
   b) Kenya
   c) South Africa

9. What should you always travel with while on Safari?
   a) A friend
   b) A parent
   c) A guide

10. Which mode of transport would typically be used on safari?
   a) Open-top bus
   b) 4x4
   c) Rickshaw

Work your way around the maze
until you reach the exit.
See if you are right by flicking to page 97.

Word wheels

Can you work out the safari animals
in the two word wheels?
See if you are right by flicking to page 97.

Left word wheel: T E O P E N L A

Right word wheel: O R D C E O C L I

Going camping

Explore this chapter on camping for fun facts and puzzles about the great outdoors.

TENTS come in all shapes and sizes, ranging from one person tents to **TEPEE STYLE,** to large tents with many rooms, to **GIGANTIC CIRCUS TENTS.**

CROSSWORDS

Crack the crosswords to enter the campsite by solving the cryptic clues below.
Answers have the same amount of letters as the number in brackets.
Can you work out the camping keyword using the letters in the shaded squares?
See if you are right by flicking to page 98.

A MAP-MAKER is called a **CARTOGRAPHER.** Modern maps use precise technology, but some of the earliest maps in history were **CAVE DRAWINGS.**

Across

1 Small bag sewn into clothing for holding things (6)
6 Give a brief description of (9)
7 Opposite of push (4)
8 Short note or reminder (4)
9 The person that lives next door to you (9)
11 Plant with stinging hairs (6)

Down

1 Put off until a future date (8)
2 Grumble; moan (8)
3 A long period of time (3)
4 Rescue vehicle at sea (8)
5 Useful asset such as oil (8)
10 Shade of a colour (3)

A COMPASS works by always pointing in the direction of the **NORTH MAGNETIC POLE,** which is not the same as the **GEOGRAPHIC NORTH POLE.**

Across
1 Position in netball: Goal _____ (6)
6 Mobile ___ : communications device (9)
7 Songbird (4)
8 Sleep in a tent (4)
9 Type of Christmas play (9)
11 Newspaper chief (6)

Down
1 Wild deer-like animal (8)
2 No rattle (anagram) (8)
3 Container for a drink (3)
4 An expert in the study of plants (8)
5 A period of 366 days (4,4)
10 Not new (3)

SUDOKUS

Solve the sudokus before slipping into your sleeping bag.
Fill in the blank squares so that numbers 1 to 6 appear once in each row,
column and 3x2 box. See if you are right by flicking to page 98.

				5	3
		2			
4					1
5	1				4
1		5	4		2
2	6				

Some sleeping
bags are called
'MUMMY BAGS'
because of their shape.
HOODS and **TAPERING
BOTTOMS** give
them a mummy-like
appearance!

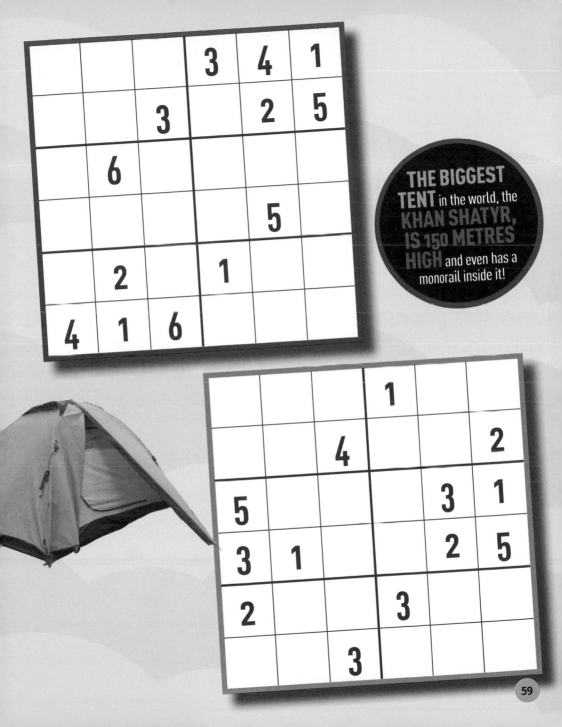

THE BIGGEST TENT in the world, the KHAN SHATYR, IS 150 METRES HIGH and even has a monorail inside it!

59

Wordsearches

Hunt through the forest for the camping terms.
Search left to right, up and down to find the words listed in the boxes below.
See if you are right by flicking to page 98.

i	l	t	f	o	r	e	s	t	z
c	p	c	f	u	l	g	s	l	d
a	l	a	n	t	e	r	n	e	x
m	l	b	o	d	t	l	q	k	p
p	i	i	b	o	o	t	s	a	r
f	j	n	p	o	a	k	h	b	t
i	b	e	y	r	m	w	i	x	a
r	u	c	k	s	a	c	k	s	a
e	k	i	n	d	p	t	e	n	t
s	a	b	e	t	o	d	f	p	k

In
**NORTH AMERICA,
TORCHES** are
commonly **KNOWN AS
FLASHLIGHTS**

boots

cabin

campfire

forest

hike

lantern

map

outdoors

rucksack

tent

n	l	v	c	h	w	u	k	x	u
a	a	s	o	w	r	t	t	h	x
h	k	x	m	i	m	o	f	u	o
a	e	x	p	l	o	r	i	n	g
y	a	u	a	d	s	a	s	t	s
c	x	i	s	l	q	n	h	i	t
r	s	s	s	i	u	g	i	n	r
p	u	f	w	f	i	e	n	g	a
s	t	o	v	e	t	r	g	v	i
q	w	t	d	t	o	y	q	r	l

compass
exploring
fishing
hunting
lake

mosquito
ranger
stove
trail
wildlife

The name 'RUCKSACK' comes from the GERMAN words 'RÜCKEN', which means 'BACK', and 'SACK', which means 'BAG'.

61

Compare the two images of camping equipment.
Can you spot the five differences between the images?
See if you are right by flicking to page 99.

As well as being used in the **GREAT OUTDOORS**, **BINOCULARS** are commonly used at the **OPERA**.

GUESS WHAT?

Can you guess the answers to the camping questions below?
Check your guesses by flicking to page 99.

1. Which of these is usually found in a first-aid kit?
   a) Bandages
   b) Bubble bath
   c) Tea bags

2. How can river water be made safe to drink?
   a) Boil it to sterilise it
   b) Leave it out in the sun for 30 minutes
   c) Mix it with fruit squash

3. Which footwear is most likely to be worn when going on a camping trip?
   a) Flippers
   b) Walking boots
   c) High heels

4. Which of these will help you get your bearings when going camping?
   a) A compass
   b) A protractor
   c) A set square

5. What are traditionally toasted around a campfire?
   a) Crisps
   b) Cereal
   c) Marshmallows

6. Which is most useful to have when camping if there are insects around?
   a) Glowsticks
   b) Flares
   c) Insect repellent

7. At the end of your camping trip, what should you do with any rubbish?
   a) Leave it lying around the campsite
   b) Take it with you
   c) Bury it at the campsite

8. What is a suitable material to burn when building a campfire?
   a) Rocks and pebbles
   b) Wet leaves
   c) Dry sticks and logs

9. What name is given to a luxurious form of camping?
   a) Glumping
   b) Glamping
   c) Skimping

10. Which of these is NOT a well-known type of tent?
    a) Dome tent
    b) Road tent
    c) Tunnel tent

Work your way around the maze to reach the exit.
See if you are right by flicking to page 99.

MAZE

Word wheels

Can you work out the camping items
in the two word wheels?
See if you are right by flicking to page 99.

At sea

All aboard for fun facts and puzzles on cruise holidays. Discover more in this chapter.

MOST CRUISE SHIPS today are at least double the size of the **TITANIC** – some are **FIVE TIMES** bigger!

CROSSWORDS

Crack the crosswords to claim your cruise ticket by solving the cryptic clues below.
Answers have the same amount of letters as the number in brackets.
Can you work out the cruise keyword using the letters in the shaded squares?
See if you are right by flicking to page 100.

CRUISE TICKETS
give access to more than just big boats: some cruise ships now have **GOLF COURSES, WATER PARKS,** and **SKY DIVE SIMULATORS!**

Across
1 Place where fish are kept (8)
5 Student at school (5)
7 A thing that takes place (5)
8 Entertain (5)
9 Exit (5)
10 Regular (8)

Down
1 Come close to (8)
2 Not liked (9)
3 Written in capital letters (5,4)
4 Excite the curiosity of (someone) (8)
6 Even (5)

SHIP TICKET
9 210 2830123436

DATE   CLASS   CRUISE

ARRIVE   DEPARTURE

CABIN
18

PRICE

0345

It's a **MYTH** that heavier **ANCHORS** are better anchors – some **MODERN** anchors are well-designed but **VERY LIGHT.**

Across

1 Sad (7)
6 Cut (grass) (3)
8 Pairs (7)
9 E.g. beetles and earwigs (7)
10 Adult female chicken (3)
11 A large cat with black spots (7)

Down

2 ___ upon Tyne: English city (9)
3 A person or company that issues books for sale (9)
4 Incredible (7)
5 Opposite of pulling (7)
7 Midday meal (5)

SUDOKUS

Solve the sudokus to set sail. Fill in the blank squares so that numbers 1 to 6 appear once in each row, column and 3x2 box. See if you are right by flicking to page 100.

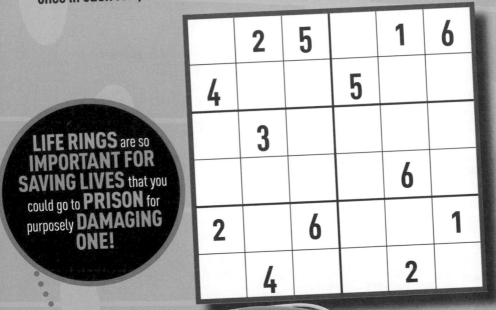

	2	5		1	6
4			5		
	3				
				6	
2		6			1
	4			2	

LIFE RINGS are so **IMPORTANT FOR SAVING LIVES** that you could go to **PRISON** for purposely **DAMAGING ONE!**

Only **MALE HUMPBACK** whales **'SING'**. The **SONG** is the **MOST COMPLEX** in the **ANIMAL KINGDOM.**

71

Wordsearches

Help the captain spot the cruise terms. Search left to right, up and down to find the words listed in the boxes below. See if you are right by flicking to page 100.

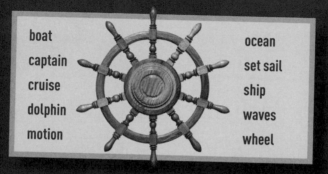

boat
captain
cruise
dolphin
motion

ocean
set sail
ship
waves
wheel

h	s	r	m	w	u	p	m	o	t
q	t	i	t	a	p	r	o	w	x
k	c	z	u	v	r	d	t	h	k
s	r	m	o	e	s	o	i	e	v
c	r	u	i	s	e	l	o	e	n
b	o	a	t	h	t	p	n	l	l
l	c	v	t	i	s	h	w	t	r
t	e	q	u	p	a	i	d	p	l
c	a	p	t	a	i	n	o	w	l
i	n	e	p	z	l	e	u	u	p

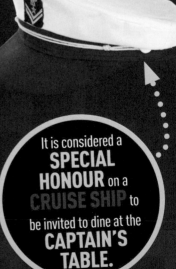

It is considered a **SPECIAL HONOUR** on a **CRUISE SHIP** to be invited to dine at the **CAPTAIN'S TABLE.**

```
m u e s s w i n d y
o w t z e t n a d a
o s a n k d a v r n
r r r n z o l i i c
n v g s b n l g f h
l l i f e b o a t o
s e a s i c k t v r
p a s s e n g e r s
a t o r f l o a t s
l i f e j a c k e t
```

anchor

drift

float

life jacket

lifeboat

moor

navigate

passengers

sea sick

windy

DOLPHINS keep one side of their **BRAIN** **'AWAKE'** when they **SLEEP** to help **CONTROL BREATHING.**

Compare the two images of the cruise ships.
Can you spot the five differences between the images?
See if you are right by flicking to page 101.

THE LONGEST CRUISE in the world takes 357 DAYS and visits ALL SEVEN CONTINENTS.

GUESS WHAT?

Can you guess the answers to the ocean questions below?
Check your guesses by flicking to page 101.

1. Which of these is a type of jellyfish?
   a) Portuguese man o' war
   b) Portuguese boy o' war
   c) Portuguese girl o' war

2. How do dolphins sleep?
   a) With one eye open to watch for predators
   b) On their back
   c) Cuddling another dolphin for heat

3. What colour is the blood of an octopus?
   a) Orange
   b) Blue
   c) Black

4. Which of these resembles a large shrimp?
   a) Plaice
   b) Pike
   c) Prawn

5. How much can a blue whale weigh?
   a) 173 tonnes
   b) 13 tonnes
   c) 103 tonnes

6. How much of the surface of the planet is ocean?
   a) Less than 30 %
   b) Less than 50 %
   c) More than 70 %

7. What name is given to the person in command of a ship?
   a) Captain
   b) Driving instructor
   c) Teacher

8. What is attached to a chain and thrown in to the sea to moor a ship?
   a) A bucket
   b) A lifeboat
   c) An anchor

9. Which of these is a type of dolphin?
   a) Cannose
   b) Bottlenose
   c) Tinnose

10. For how long have jellyfish been found in the planet's seas?
    a) 1 million years
    b) 10 million years
    c) At least 500 million years

MAZE

Work your way around the maze until you reach the exit. See if you are right by flicking to page 101.

Word wheels

Can you work out the cruising words in the two word wheels?
See if you are right by flicking to page 101.

Landmarks

Keep your eyes peeled for spectacular sights, fun facts and puzzles about famous landmarks in this chapter.

It takes a team of **25 PAINTERS**, with **60 TONNES OF PAINT** and **1,500 BRUSHES**, **18 MONTHS** to repaint the **EIFFEL TOWER**.

CROSSWORDS

Crack the crossword to start Big Ben's chimes by solving the cryptic clues below.
Answers have the same amount of letters as the number in brackets.
Can you work out the landmark keyword using the letters in the shaded squares?
See if you are right by flicking to page 102.

BIG BEN'S HOURLY CHIMING is now silenced for **FOUR YEARS** due to maintenance work and won't be heard again until **2021**.

Across
4 Threatening; hazardous (9)
6 Mediterranean ___ : large body of water (3)
8 Impressive bird of prey (5)
9 Not before (5)
10 Opposite of bottom (3)
12 List of lessons and when they happen (9)

Down
1 Possess; own (4)
2 Acknowledge a significant date such as your birthday (9)
3 Fail to remember (6)
5 Farm animals (5)
6 Clever (5)
7 Season when leaves fall from trees (6)
11 Solely; merely (4)

(3,3)

Across

1. Do away with (7)
6. Tree with needle-shaped leaves (3)
8. Alters (7)
9. Place providing higher education (7)
10. Hot drink (3)
11. Leader of a football team (7)

Down

2. A city in Spain (9)
3. Type of pasta in thin strings (9)
4. Person in the army (7)
5. In place of something else (7)
7. Where one finds Cardiff (5)

BUCKINGHAM PALACE has 775 rooms, including 92 offices, 52 royal bedrooms, 188 staff bedrooms, and 78 bathrooms!

SUDOKUS

Solve the sudokus to enter the colosseum.
Fill in the blank squares so that numbers 1 to 6 appear once in each row,
column and 3x2 box. See if you are right by flicking to page 102.

Between **1999** and **2001,** engineers had to work on the TOWER OF PISA because it was leaning so far it could've fallen over!

			4		
5			1		
3			2		5
2					4
		2		4	3
4		6			

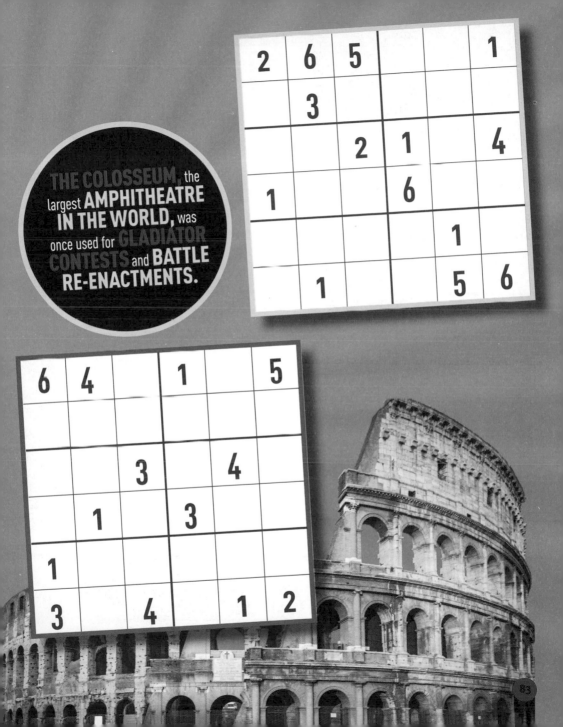

2	6	5			1
	3				
		2	1		4
1			6		
				1	
	1			5	6

THE COLOSSEUM, the largest **AMPHITHEATRE IN THE WORLD,** was once used for **GLADIATOR CONTESTS** and **BATTLE RE-ENACTMENTS.**

6	4		1		5
		3		4	
	1		3		
1					
3		4		1	2

Wordsearches

Set off on a round-the-world tour to spot the famous landmarks.
Search left to right, up and down to find the words listed in the boxes below.
See if you are right by flicking to page 102.

a	n	g	k	o	r	w	a	t	i
b	t	a	j	m	a	h	a	l	a
i	w	r	k	p	l	i	q	t	m
g	u	l	u	r	u	t	s	o	u
b	p	a	r	t	h	e	n	o	n
e	a	r	r	v	m	h	j	f	i
n	a	c	r	o	p	o	l	i	s
m	o	u	n	t	f	u	j	i	l
j	c	o	l	o	s	s	e	u	m
s	t	o	n	e	h	e	n	g	e

HISTORIANS still aren't sure exactly how the **PYRAMIDS OF GIZA** were built, though they estimate construction took nearly **20 YEARS!**

Acropolis

Angkor Wat

Big Ben

Colosseum

Mount Fuji

Parthenon

Stonehenge

Taj Mahal

Uluru

White House

e n u v z l s b t m
z o t e s o a p o a
e t h r c n c y k t
w r e s n d r r y t
r e l a t o e a o e
z d o i o n c m t r
i a u l w e o i o h
s m v l e y e d w o
x e r e r e u s e r
t h e s h a r d r n

THE TAJ MAHAL is a white marble palace built as a **TOMB** for the **WIFE OF MUGHAL EMPEROR, SHAH JAHAN.**

CN Tower
London Eye
Matterhorn
Notre-dame
Pyramids

Sacre-coeur
The Louvre
The Shard
Tokyo Tower
Versailles

85

CLOSE UP

Match the mind-boggling magnifications to the named pictures opposite. See if you are right by flicking to page 103.

1

2

3

4

5

6

Burj al Arab

1

Leaning Tower of Pisa

2

Pyramids of Giza

3

Big Ben

4

Taj Mahal

5

Statue of Liberty

6

GUESS WHAT?

Can you guess the answers to the landmark questions below?
Check your guesses by flicking to page 103.

1. How many capsules are there on the London Eye?
   a) 12
   b) 96
   c) 32

2. Where is the Louvre Museum located?
   a) Budapest
   b) Sydney
   c) Paris

3. What does the Statue of Liberty hold in her hand above her head?
   a) A torch
   b) A trophy
   c) A flower

4. How tall is The Shard building in London?
   a) 510 metres
   b) 210 metres
   c) 310 metres

5. Stonehenge is a famous prehistoric monument. Where is it found?
   a) Scotland
   b) Ireland
   c) England

6. Where would you find the Taj Mahal?
   a) Sri Lanka
   b) India
   c) Tunisia

7. Which of these is a famous London landmark?
   a) Big Ken
   b) Big Ben
   c) Big Len

8. Who lives at the White House?
   a) The US President
   b) The Prime Minister
   c) The Queen

9. Fill in the blank: the ____ Tower of Pisa
   a) Bending
   b) Leaning
   c) Curving

10. In which country would you find the Great Pyramid of Giza?
    a) Namibia
    b) Thailand
    c) Egypt

MAZE

Work your way around the maze until you reach the exit. See if you are right by flicking to page 103.

Word wheels

Can you work out the landmarks in the two word wheels?
See if you are right by flicking to page 103.

Solutions

Crosswords

Keyword: MAP

Keyword: PETROL

Sudokus

1	6	3	4	5	2
5	2	4	1	3	6
3	1	6	2	4	5
4	5	2	3	6	1
6	4	1	5	2	3
2	3	5	6	1	4

3	4	1	6	5	2
6	2	5	3	4	1
5	1	6	4	2	3
4	3	2	5	1	6
1	5	3	2	6	4
2	6	4	1	3	5

2	5	3	1	6	4
4	6	1	2	5	3
5	1	2	4	3	6
3	4	6	5	2	1
1	3	5	6	4	2
6	2	4	3	1	5

Wordsearches

Spot the difference

Guess what?

1) b – Passport   2) a – In the hold   3) b – 5

4) c – Hartsfield–Jackson Atlanta International

5) a – 75.7 million   6) a – Saba Airport, Caribbean

7) c – Roof rack   8) a – Satellites

9) c – Departure boards   10) b – Conductor

Maze

Word wheels

Passport, Ticket

Solutions

Page 20–21

Crosswords

Keyword: BUCKET

Keyword: SPADE

Crossword 1 (left):
- MOTORBIKE (with vertical crossings)
- M E A N / F L E A
- ADDRESS
- PICTURE
- SIXTEEN
- ADVENTURE

Crossword 2 (right):
- NETBALL
- VAGUE
- LOWERCASE
- CORGIS
- SPECIES

Page 22–23

Sudokus

Sudoku 1:
5	6	3	1	2	4
2	1	4	5	3	6
1	3	2	4	6	5
6	4	5	2	1	3
4	2	6	3	5	1
3	5	1	6	4	2

Sudoku 2:
1	2	4	3	5	6
5	6	3	2	1	4
6	3	5	4	2	1
2	4	1	5	6	3
3	1	2	6	4	5
4	5	6	1	3	2

Sudoku 3:
1	4	5	3	2	6
6	3	2	4	1	5
3	2	4	5	6	1
5	1	6	2	4	3
2	6	3	1	5	4
4	5	1	6	3	2

Page 24–25

Wordsearches

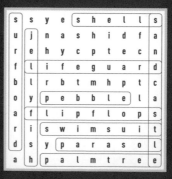

Wordsearch 1:
s	g	d	h	b	r	a	x	s	j
u	t	e	r	e	u	v	b	a	q
n	q	c	t	a	b	i	g	n	o
b	b	k	x	c	b	c	l	d	h
l	u	c	s	h	e	l	a	a	e
o	c	h	t	e	r	c	s	s	s
c	k	a	o	r	r	i	a	n	p
k	e	i	o	w	i	e	l	e	a
x	t	r	c	e	n	n	s	q	d
l	i	l	o	l	g	m	a	l	e

Wordsearch 2:
s	s	y	e	s	h	e	l	l	s	s
u	j	n	a	s	h	i	d	f	a	a
r	e	h	y	c	p	t	e	c	n	n
f	l	i	f	e	g	u	a	r	d	d
b	l	r	b	t	m	h	p	t	c	c
o	o	p	e	b	b	l	e	l	a	a
a	f	l	i	p	f	l	o	p	s	s
r	i	s	w	i	m	s	u	i	t	t
d	s	y	p	a	r	a	s	o	l	l
a	h	p	a	l	m	t	r	e	e	e

Page 26–27

Spot the difference

Page 28–29

Guess what?

1) c – A safe and clean beach
2) a – A pod
3) b – A cone
4) a – To shield you from the sun
5) a – UV rays from the sun
6) c – Newquay
7) c – Sandcastles
8) c – 5
9) a – Rock pool
10) b – Surfing

Maze

Word wheels

Beachball, Snorkel

Solutions

Page 32–33

Crosswords

C	H	R	I	S	T	M	A	S	
O				O				W	
P	U	D	D	I	N	G		I	M
Y		E		I		I		M	
	V	I	N	E	G	A	R		
C		T		H			S		
O		D	I	S	T	A	N	T	
M		S					A		
B	U	T	T	E	R	F	L	Y	

Keyword: THEATRE

I	N	F	O	R	M	A	L		
N		I			R		G	D	
D	I	R	T	Y		O	I	
U		E		O	P	E	N	S	
S		W		U		N		S	
T	H	O	R	N		T		O	
R		R		G	R	I	L	L	
Y		K				N		V	
	E	S	T	I	M	A	T	E	

Keyword: UNDERGROUND

Page 34–35

Sudokus

5	4	1	3	2	6
3	6	2	1	4	5
6	5	4	2	1	3
1	2	3	5	6	4
4	1	5	6	3	2
2	3	6	4	5	1

4	6	5	3	2	1
2	1	3	5	4	6
3	2	6	1	5	4
5	4	1	6	3	2
1	5	2	4	6	3
6	3	4	2	1	5

5	6	4	3	1	2
2	3	1	5	6	4
3	4	5	1	2	6
1	2	6	4	5	3
4	5	2	6	3	1
6	1	3	2	4	5

Page 36–37

Wordsearches

a	g	v	t	c	s	f	s	a	c
c	n	i	o	u	m	e	t	r	o
a	a	e	u	l	e	m	m	l	f
m	r	w	r	t	d	o	u	u	f
e	j	p	b	u	a	n	s	l	e
r	t	o	u	r	g	u	i	d	e
a	v	i	s	e	m	m	g	s	s
p	u	n	o	k	q	e	h	t	u
i	r	t	d	g	d	n	t	y	y
t	o	u	r	i	s	t	s	m	k

u	w	a	l	k	i	n	g	z	q
a	c	r	o	w	d	s	m	o	p
r	s	o	u	v	e	n	i	r	s
e	x	p	e	r	i	e	n	c	e
s	d	s	h	o	p	p	i	n	g
e	s	s	b	t	h	e	b	i	s
a	a	t	h	i	p	e	r	m	c
r	c	a	f	e	u	r	e	c	r
c	t	l	a	n	d	m	a	r	k
h	p	i	c	n	i	c	k	o	u

Spot the difference

Guess what?

1) b – Metro   2) c – Tour guide   3) c – Central Park
4) c – Berlin   5) c – Venice   6) c– Black
7) c – £2,600   8) c – Macy's   9) c – The big apple
10) a – Paris

Maze

Word wheels

Shopping, Theatre

Solutions

Crosswords

Crossword 1:

	J		H			G	
B	E	C	O	M	E		E	
	W		M		L	O	O	K
	E		E		E		G	
C	L	A	W		C	U	R	E
	L		O		T		A	
P	E	A	R		R		P	
	R		K	N	I	G	H	T
	Y				C		Y	

Keyword: CHEETAH

Crossword 2:

	S		N				S	
A	C	R	O	S	S		C	
	A		N		E	X	I	T
	R		S		N		E	
H	E	R	E		T	I	N	Y
	C		N		E		T	
A	R	M	S		N		I	
	O			E	X	C	U	S	E
	W				E		T	

Keyword: RHINO

Sudokus

Sudoku 1:

4	2	6	1	5	3
1	3	5	2	4	6
6	5	2	3	1	4
3	1	4	5	6	2
5	4	3	6	2	1
2	6	1	4	3	5

Sudoku 2:

3	1	6	4	2	5
2	5	4	6	3	1
4	3	5	2	1	6
1	6	2	5	4	3
6	4	1	3	5	2
5	2	3	1	6	4

Sudoku 3:

6	2	1	3	5	4
4	3	5	6	1	2
3	4	6	5	2	1
5	1	2	4	3	6
2	5	4	1	6	3
1	6	3	2	4	5

Wordsearches

Wordsearch 1:

```
q e k n z k r r u a
o s l o s t x e a b
s l m e e r k a t a
g o r i l l a d p l
j t c h e e t a h w
c h t j p a r r o t
t d r h i n o r v
s g i r a f f e s s
g h y e n a r r e t
u e a n t e l o p e
```

Wordsearch 2:

```
r w e v r s z q c s
g a z e l l e d i f
c r o c o d i l e a
t t s m o n k e y f
s h t b a b o o n x
i o r v i e h p x z
a g i d o s n a k e
s o c a z b f r u b
q o h l i o n d n r
p x s s u l k t s a
```

Close Up

Page 50–51

1 – 4 Elephant   2 – 3 Giraffe   3 – 1 Lion

4 – 6 Crocodile   5 – 2 Zebra   6 – 5 Flamingo

Guess what?

Page 52–53

1) c – Their natural environment   2) a – Black and white

3) a – Cheetah   4) b – Giraffe   5) c – Cows

6) c – Kenya   7) c – A pride   8) c – South Africa

9) c – A guide   10) b – 4x4

Maze

Word wheels

Antelope, Crocodile

Solutions

Page 56–57

Crosswords

Crossword 1:

P	O	C	K	E	T		
O		O		R		L	R
S	U	M	M	A	R	I	S	E
T		P		F		S	S
P	U	L	L		M	E	M	O
O		A			B		O
N	E	I	G	H	B	O	U	R
E		N		U		A	C
		N	E	T	T	L	E

Keyword: HIKING

Crossword 2:

A	T	T	A	C	K		
N		O		U		B	L
T	E	L	E	P	H	O	N	E
E		E				T	A
L	A	R	K		C	A	M	P
O		A				N	Y
P	A	N	T	O	M	I	M	E
E		T		L		S	A
	E	D	I	T	O	R

Keyword: RUCKSACK

Page 58–59

Sudokus

Sudoku 1:

6	4	1	2	5	3
3	5	2	1	4	6
4	2	6	5	3	1
5	1	3	6	2	4
1	3	5	4	6	2
2	6	4	3	1	5

Sudoku 2:

6	5	2	3	4	1
1	4	3	6	2	5
5	6	4	2	1	3
2	3	1	4	5	6
3	2	5	1	6	4
4	1	6	5	3	2

Sudoku 3:

6	2	5	1	4	3
1	3	4	5	6	2
5	4	2	6	3	1
3	1	6	4	2	5
2	6	1	3	5	4
4	5	3	2	1	6

Page 60–61

Wordsearches

Wordsearch 1:

i	l	t	f	o	r	e	s	t	z
c	p	c	f	u	l	g	s	l	d
a	l	a	n	t	e	r	n	e	x
m	l	b	o	d	t	l	q	k	p
p	i	i	b	o	o	t	s	a	r
f	j	n	p	o	a	k	h	b	t
i	b	e	y	r	m	w	i	x	a
r	u	c	k	s	a	c	k	s	a
e	k	i	n	d	p	t	e	n	t
s	a	b	e	t	o	d	f	p	k

Wordsearch 2:

n	l	v	c	h	w	u	k	x	u
a	a	s	o	w	r	t	t	h	x
h	k	x	m	i	m	o	f	u	o
a	e	x	p	l	o	r	i	n	g
y	a	u	a	d	s	a	s	t	i
c	x	i	s	l	q	n	h	i	n
r	s	s	i	l	i	u	g	n	g
p	u	f	w	f	i	e	n	g	v
s	t	o	v	e	t	o	y	q	l
q	w	t	d	t	o	y	q	r	l

98

Spot the difference

Guess what?

1) a – Bandage

2) a – Boil it to sterilise it

3) b – Walking boots

4) a – A compass

5) c – Marshmallows

6) c – Insect repellent

7) b – Take it with you

8) c – Dry sticks and logs

9) b – Glamping

10) b – Road tent

Maze

Word wheels

Marshmallow,
Rucksack

Solutions

Crosswords

Keyword: CAPTAIN

Keyword: DOLPHIN

Sudokus

3	2	5	4	1	6
4	6	1	5	3	2
6	3	2	1	5	4
5	1	4	2	6	3
2	5	6	3	4	1
1	4	3	6	2	5

1	4	2	5	6	3
3	5	6	2	1	4
5	2	3	1	4	6
4	6	1	3	5	2
2	1	4	6	3	5
6	3	5	4	2	1

5	6	3	2	1	4
4	1	2	3	6	5
2	4	5	6	3	1
6	3	1	5	4	2
1	2	6	4	5	3
3	5	4	1	2	6

Wordsearches

Spot the difference

Guess what?

1) a– Portuguese man o' war
2) a – With one eye open to watch for predators
3) b – Blue   4) c – Prawn   5) a – 173 tonnes
6) c – More than 70 %   7) a– Captain   8) c – An anchor
9) b – Bottlenose   10) c – At least 500 million years

Maze

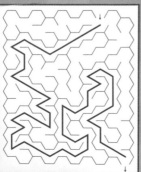

Word wheels
Anchor, Captain

Solutions

Crosswords

```
    H   C   F
D A N G E R O U S
    V   L   R   H
S E A   E A G L E
M   U   B   E   E
A F T E R   T O P
R   U   A   N
T I M E T A B L E
    N   E   Y
```
Keyword: BIG BEN

```
  A B O L I S H
O   A       P   I
F I R   W   A   N
F   C H A N G E S
I   E   L   H   T
C O L L E G E   E
E   O   S   T E A
R   N       T   D
  C A P T A I N
```
Keyword: TOWER BRIDGE

Sudokus

6	1	3	4	5	2
5	2	4	1	3	6
3	4	1	2	6	5
2	6	5	3	1	4
1	5	2	6	4	3
4	3	6	5	2	1

2	6	5	3	4	1
4	3	1	5	6	2
6	5	2	1	3	4
1	4	3	6	2	5
5	2	6	4	1	3
3	1	4	2	5	6

6	4	2	1	3	5
5	3	1	2	6	4
2	6	3	5	4	1
4	1	5	3	2	6
1	2	6	4	5	3
3	5	4	6	1	2

Wordsearches

```
a n g k o r w a t i
b t a j m a h a l a
i w r k p l i q t m
g u l u r u t s o u
b p a r t h e n o n
e a r r v m h j f i
n a c r o p o l i s
m o u n t f u j i l
j c o l o s s e u m
s t o n e h e n g e
```

```
e n u v z l s b t m
z o t e s o a p o a
e t h r c n c y k t
w r e s n d r r y t
r e l a t o e a o e
z d o i o n c m t r
i a u l l e e o o h
s m v l e y e i w o
x e r e r e u d e r
t h e s h a r d r n
```

Close Up

Page 86–87

1 – 6 Statue of Liberty   2 – 5 Taj Mahal

3 – 4 Big Ben   4 – 1 Burj al Arab

5 – 3 Pyramids of Giza   6 – 2 Leaning Tower of Pisa

Guess what?

Page 88–89

1) c – 32   2) c – Paris   3) a – A torch

4) c – 310 metres   5) c – England   6) b – India

7) b – Big Ben   8) a – The US President

9) b – Leaning   10) c – Egypt

Maze

Word wheels

Colosseum, Stonehenge

SUBSCRIBE TODAY!

Visit our new website natgeokids.com

Love National Geographic Kids? Have you enjoyed our free sample iPad edition from the App Store? Well, sign up to the magazine, iPad edition or BOTH today and save money!

PRINT ONLY

£30

A subscription to **National Geographic Kids magazine** is the perfect gift for boys and girls aged six and over. Packed with features about nature, science, geography, history and popular culture, Nat Geo Kids gets children excited about the world. It helps with their homework, too!

FULL SUBSCRIPTION

PREMIUM

£40

This **premium package** will keep kids entertained for hours while teaching them about the amazing world we live in. Subscribe to both **National Geographic Kids magazine** and the interactive **Nat Geo Kids iPad app** and you'll save £25!

DIGITAL ONLY

£20

The **National Geographic Kids iPad app** is jam-packed with videos, games, sounds and extra interactive content that really bring **National Geographic Kids magazine** to life! Engaging and exciting, **Nat Geo Kids' iPad edition** makes learning more fun than ever!